MOVIE & TV THEMES
PLAYALONG SOLOS FOR VIOLIN

	PAGE NUMBER	CD TRACK NUMBER
A Whole New World	2	1
Circle Of Life	4	2
Love Is All Around	6	3
Moon River	8	4
Theme from "Schindler's List"	10	5
Theme from Star Trek®	11	6
Take My Breath Away	12	7
Theme from the Godfather	14	8
Up Where We Belong	15	9
Love Story	16	10
You Must Love Me	17	11
Where Everybody Knows Your Name	18	12
B♭ Tuning Notes		13
A Tuning Notes		14

Arrangements by Jack Long

HOW TO USE THE CD ACCOMPANIMENT:

A melody cue appears on the right channel only. If your CD player has a balance adjustment, you can adjust the volume of the melody by turning down the right channel.

ISBN 0-634-00463-8

HAL•LEONARD® CORPORATION

7777 W. BLUEMOUND RD. P.O. BOX 13819 MILWAUKEE, WI 53213

Visit Hal Leonard Online at
www.halleonard.com

A WHOLE NEW WORLD

from Walt Disney's ALLADDIN

VIOLIN

Music by ALAN MENKEN
Lyrics by TIM RICE

CIRCLE OF LIFE ♦2

from Walt Disney Pictures' THE LION KING

Music by ELTON JOHN
Lyrics by TIM RICE

VIOLIN

Medium slow tempo (♩ = 88)

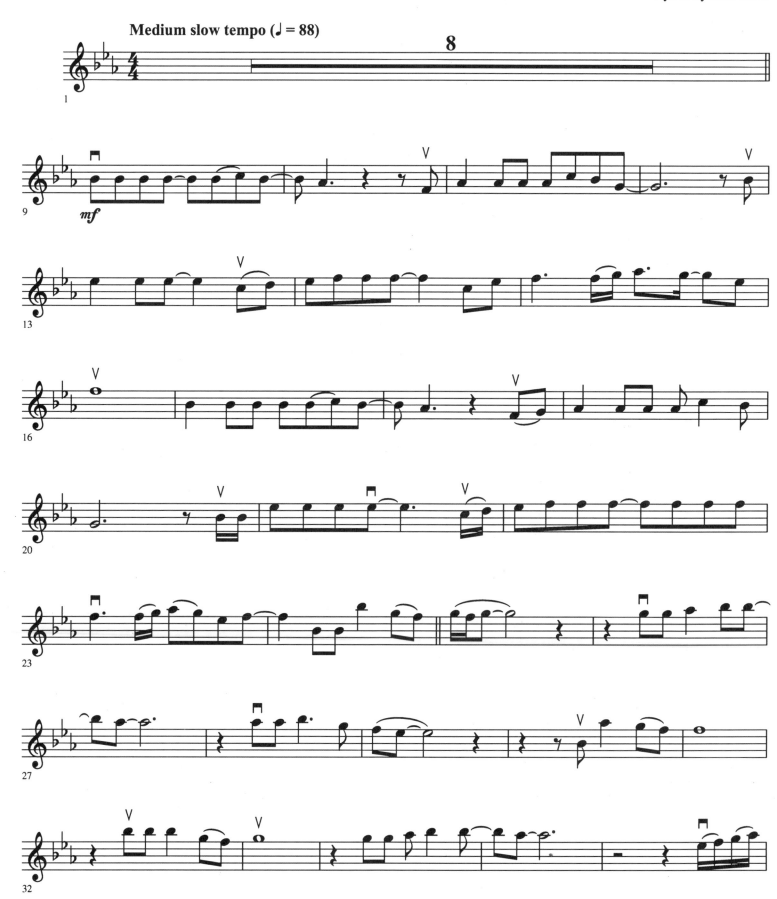

6

LOVE IS ALL AROUND ◆③

featured on the Motion Picture Soundtrack FOUR WEDDINGS AND A FUNERAL

Words and Music by
REG PRESLEY

VIOLIN

MOON RIVER

from the Paramount Picture BREAKFAST AT TIFFANY'S

Words by JOHNNY MERCER
Music by HENRY MANCINI

VIOLIN

Theme From "SCHINDLER'S LIST" ◆5

from the Universal Motion Picture SCHINDLER'S LIST

Composed by JOHN WILLIAMS

VIOLIN

Theme From "STAR TREK®"

from the Paramount Television Series STAR TREK

Words by GENE RODDENBERRY
Music by ALEXANDER COURAGE

VIOLIN

TAKE MY BREATH AWAY ◆7

(Love Theme)
from the Paramount Picture TOP GUN

VIOLIN

Words and Music by
GIORGIO MORODER and TOM WHITLOCK

THE GODFATHER ◆8

(Love Theme)

from the Paramount Picture THE GODFATHER

By NINO ROTA

VIOLIN

UP WHERE WE BELONG

from the Paramount Picture AN OFFICER AND A GENTLEMAN

Words by WILL JENNINGS
Music by BUFFY SAINTE-MARIE and JACK NITZSCHE

VIOLIN

LOVE STORY ◆10

Theme from the Paramount Picture LOVE STORY

VIOLIN

Music by FRANCIS LAI

YOU MUST LOVE ME 11

from the Cinergi Motion Picture EVITA

Words by TIM RICE
Music by ANDREW LLOYD WEBBER

VIOLIN

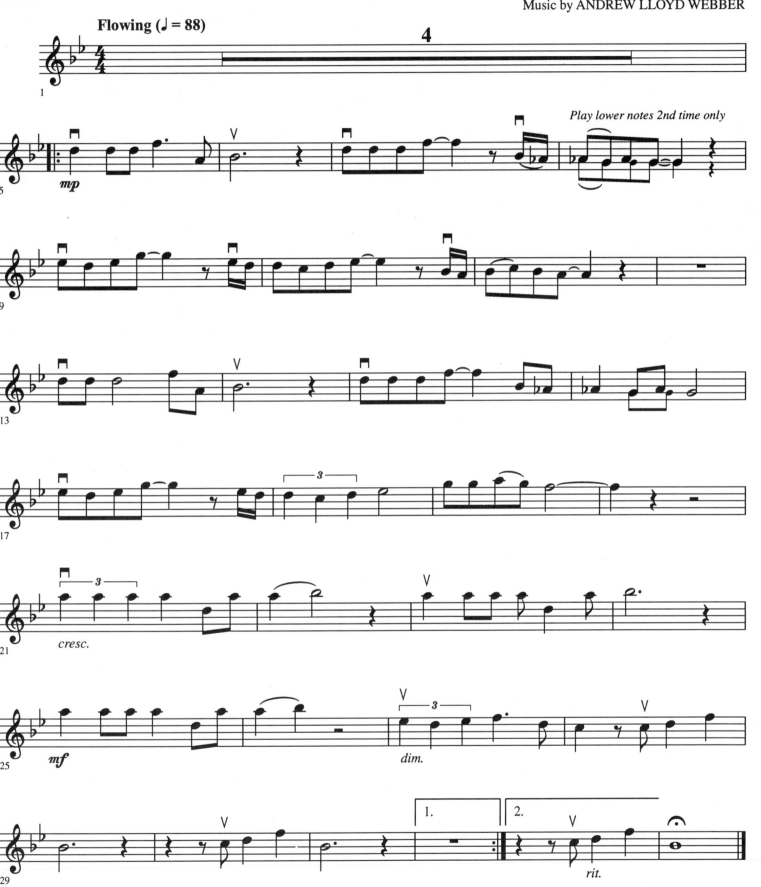

WHERE EVERYBODY KNOWS YOUR NAME

Theme from the Paramount Television Series CHEERS

VIOLIN

Words and Music by
GARY PORTNOY and JUDY HART ANGELO

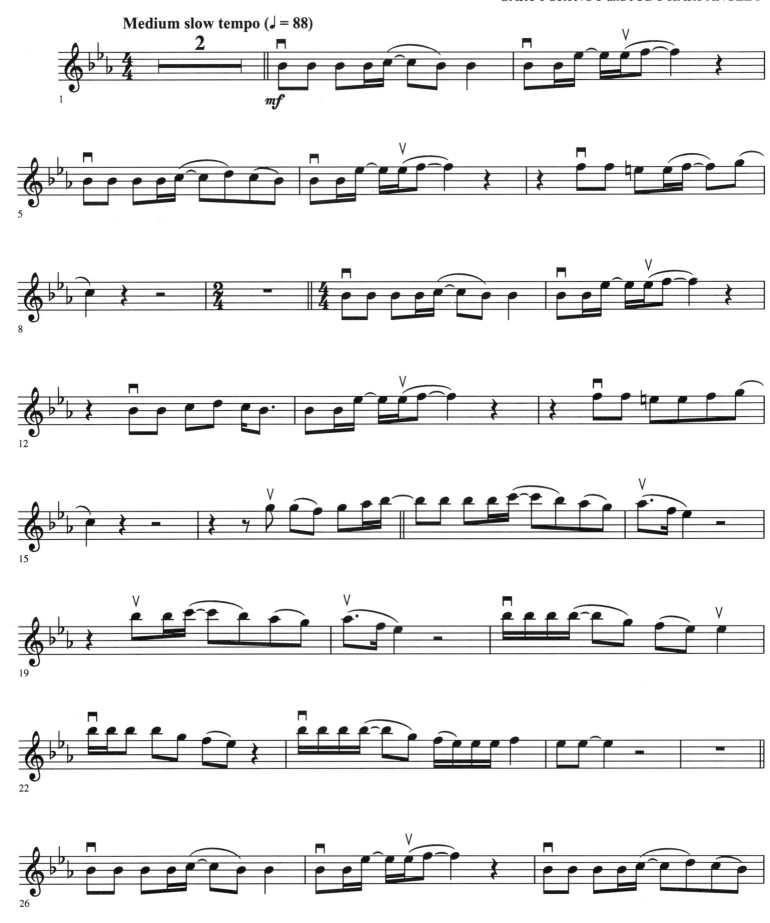

PLAY MORE OF YOUR FAVORITE SONGS
WITH GREAT INSTRUMENTAL FOLIOS FROM HAL LEONARD

Best of the Beatles
89 of the greatest songs from the legends of Liverpool, including: All You Need Is Love • And I Love Her • The Fool on the Hill • Got to Get You into My Life • Here, There, and Everywhere • Let It Be • Norwegian Wood • Something • Ticket to Ride • and more.

00847217 Flute $9.95
00847218 Clarinet...................................$9.95
00847219 Alto Sax..................................$9.95
00847220 Trumpet $9.95
00847221 Trombone................................$9.95

Broadway Showstoppers
47 incredible selections from over 25 shows. Songs include: All I Ask of You • Cabaret • Camelot • Climb Ev'ry Mountain • Comedy Tonight • Don't Cry for Me Argentina • Hello, Dolly! • I Dreamed a Dream • Maria • Memory • Oklahoma! • Seventy-Six Trombones • and many more!

08721339 Flute $6.95
08721340 Bb Clarinet.............................$6.95
08721341 Eb Alto Sax.............................$6.95
08721342 Bb Trumpet/Bb Tenor Sax $6.95
08721343 Trombone (Bass Clef Instruments) $6.95

Choice Jazz Standards
30 songs, including: All the Things You Are • A Foggy Day • The Girl From Ipanema • Just in Time • My Funny Valentine • Quiet Nights of Quiet Stars • Smoke Gets in Your Eyes • Watch What Happens • and many more.

00850276 Flute $5.95
00850275 Clarinet...................................$5.95
00850274 Alto Sax..................................$5.95
00850273 Trumpet $5.95
00850272 Trombone................................$5.95

Classic Rock & Roll
31 songs, including: Blue Suede Shoes • Blueberry Hill • Dream Lover • I Want to Hold Your Hand • The Shoop Shoop Song • Surfin' U.S.A. • and many others.

00850248 Flute $5.95
00850249 Clarinet...................................$5.95
00850250 Alto Sax..................................$5.95
00850251 Trumpet $5.95
00850252 Trombone................................$5.95

FOR MORE INFORMATION, SEE YOUR LOCAL MUSIC DEALER, OR WRITE TO:

HAL•LEONARD CORPORATION
7777 W. BLUEMOUND RD. P.O. BOX 13819 MILWAUKEE, WI 53213

Prices, contents, and availability subject to change without notice.
Disney characters and artwork © The Walt Disney Company.

The Definitive Jazz Collection
88 songs, including: Ain't Misbehavin' • All the Things You Are • Birdland • Body and Soul • A Foggy Day • Girl From Ipanema • Love for Sale • Mercy, Mercy, Mercy • Moonlight in Vermont • Night and Day • Skylark • Stormy Weather • and more.

08721673 Flute $9.95
08721674 Clarinet...................................$9.95
08721675 Alto Sax..................................$9.95
08721676 Trumpet $9.95
08721677 Trombone $9.95

Definitive Rock 'n' Roll Collection
95 classics, including: Barbara Ann • Blue Suede Shoes • Blueberry Hill • Duke of Earl • Earth Angel • Gloria • The Lion Sleeps Tonight • Louie, Louie • My Boyfriend's Back • Rock Around the Clock • Stand by Me • The Twist • Wild Thing • and more!

00847207 Flute $9.95
00847208 Clarinet...................................$9.95
00847209 Alto Sax $9.95
00847210 Trumpet $9.95
00847211 Trombone $9.95

Disney's The Lion King
5 fun solos for students from Disney's blockbuster. Includes: Can You Feel the Love Tonight • Circle of Life • Hakuna Matata • I Just Can't Wait to Be King • Be Prepared.

00849949 Flute $5.95
00849950 Clarinet...................................$5.95
00849951 Alto Sax...................................$5.95
00849952 Trumpet $5.95
00849953 Trombone $5.95
00849955 Piano Accompaniment $9.95
00849003 Easy Violin $5.95
00849004 Viola $5.95
00849005 Cello $5.95

Best of Andrew Lloyd Webber
26 of his best, including: All I Ask of You • Close Every Door • Don't Cry for Me Argentina • I Don't Know How to Love Him • Love Changes Everything • Memory • and more.

00849939 Flute $6.95
00849940 Clarinet...................................$6.95
00849941 Trumpet $6.95
00849942 Alto Sax...................................$6.95
00849943 Trombone $6.95
00849015 Violin $6.95

BOOK/CD PLAY-ALONG PACKS

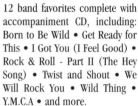

Band Jam
Book/CD Packs
12 band favorites complete with accompaniment CD, including: Born to Be Wild • Get Ready for This • I Got You (I Feel Good) • Rock & Roll - Part II (The Hey Song) • Twist and Shout • We Will Rock You • Wild Thing • Y.M.C.A • and more.

00841232 Flute..$10.95
00841233 Clarinet $10.95
00841234 Alto Sax...................................$10.95
00841235 Trumpet....................................$10.95
00841236 Horn $10.95
00841237 Trombone $10.95
00841238 Violin.......................................$10.95

Favorite Movie Themes
Book/CD Packs
13 themes, including: An American Symphony • Braveheart - Main Title • Chariots of Fire • Forrest Gump - Main Title • Theme from Jurrasic Park • Mission: Impossible Theme • and more.

00841166 Flute...$10.95
00841167 Clarinet.....................................$10.95
00841168 Trumpet/Tenor Sax $10.95
00841169 Alto Sax....................................$10.95
00841170 Trombone..................................$10.95
00841171 French Horn..............................$10.95

Hymns for the Master
Book/CD Packs
15 inspirational favorites, including: All, Hail the Power of Jesus' Name • Amazing Grace • Crown Him With Many Crowns • Joyful, Joyful We Adore Thee • This Is My Father's World • When I Survey the Wondrous Cross • and more.

00841136 Flute...$12.95
00841137 Clarinet.....................................$12.95
00841138 Alto Sax....................................$12.95
00841139 Trumpet.....................................$12.95
00841140 Trombone..................................$12.95

My Heart Will Go On
Instrumental Solo Book/CD Pack
This arrangement of Celine Dion's mega-hit features a solo part for instrumentalists to play with a real orchestral background that sounds exactly like the original!

00841308 Solo for Flute, Clarinet, Alto Sax, Tenor Sax, Trumpet, Horn or Trombone.................$6.95
00841309 Solo for Violin, Viola or Cello $6.95

0299